AF408379

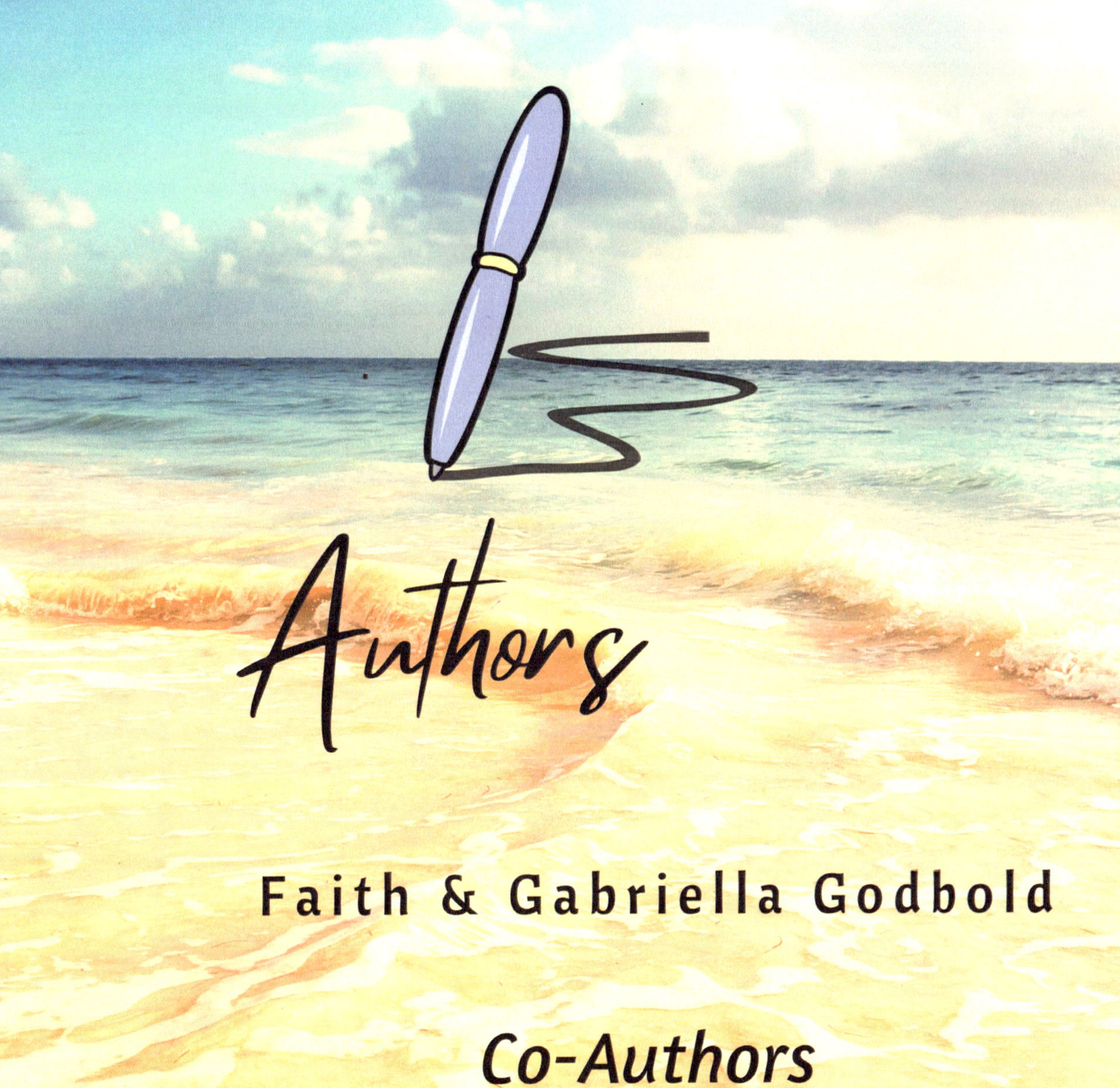

# Authors

Faith & Gabriella Godbold

## Co-Authors

Temico & Stephanie Godbold

## Illustrators

Aqib Saleem
Temico Godbold
Faith Godbold
Gabriella Godbold

# Presented By

*Please Visit Our Website*
- Sisters saving species foundation.org

# Faith & Gabriella's Madagascar Super Hero Adventure



| | |
|---|---|
| 1 RED FODY | 7 GOLDEN MANTELLA |
| 2 TOMATO FROG | 8 SATANIC LEAF-TAILED GECKO |
| 3 FIERCE FOSSA | 9 LEAF-NOSED SNAKE |
| 4 COMET MOTH | 10 GIRAFFE WEEVIL |
| 5 PANTHER CHAMELEON | 11 AYE-AYE |
| 6 RADIATED TORTOISE | 12 BLUE COUA |

# Introduction

"Faith & Gabriella's Madagascar Super Hero Adventure" takes readers on an educational journey through the unique wildlife of Madagascar, narrated by two young sisters. As they meet the superhero Aye-Eye Man, they learn about the threats facing endangered animals due to deforestation. With colorful illustrations and factual storytelling, the book introduces 12 native species, from the Golden Mantella to the Radiated Tortoise. Each animal's habitat, behavior, and conservation status are explored, encouraging readers to appreciate and protect the biodiversity. Through their adventure, Faith and Gabriella inspire curiosity and compassion for the natural world, while highlighting the importance of environmental stewardship. With heartfelt thanks to their supportive family and friends, the book serves as both an educational tool and a celebration of teamwork and dedication.

# WELCOME TO
# GREAT RED ISLAND

Hi there! We're Faith and Gabriella, and we're thrilled to invite you on an exciting adventure to the magical island of Madagascar! Have you ever imagined a place where the animals are so unique, they can't be found anywhere else on Earth? That's Madagascar for you!

Today, we're not alone on this journey. We're accompanied by Aye-Eye Man. With his amazing powers, he protects the forests and animals of Madagascar from the dangers of deforestation.

As we explore this island, we will meet 12 extraordinary animals that are endangered and in need of our help. From the tiny Tomato Frog to the mysterious Blue Coua, each creature has a special story to tell.

But there's a problem: deforestation. When trees are cut down, these animals lose their homes and food sources. The Aye-Eye Man will help us understand how we can all pitch in to protect these wonderful creatures and their habitats.

So, put on your explorer hats and join us as we dive into the wonders of Madagascar. Together, we'll discover the beauty of its wildlife and learn how to become heroes for these endangered animals. Ready? Let's explore this super adventure together!

Faith and Gabriella

# PROTECT
## THE ENDANGERED ANIMALS
### IN MADAGASCAR

Madagascar is home to over 100 endangered species, including the Aye-Aye, Fossa, and Radiated Tortoise. Habitat loss due to deforestation and climate change are major threats to their survival. Conservation efforts are crucial to protect these unique animals from extinction.

# AYE-EYE MAN

Introducing Super Hero Aye-Eye Man! A dedicated guardian committed to protect Madagascar from deforestation and habitat loss. With his superpowers, Aye-Eye Man ensures that every species, big or small, beautiful or weird, plays its unique role in maintaining the Earth's health and balance. His mission is to preserve all species and highlight the importance of biodiversity.

Aye-Eye Man inspires us all to appreciate and safeguard nature's incredible creations. On this adventure, Aye-Eye Man will introduce us to 12 amazing animals that are at risk of disappearing forever. He'll share fascinating facts about them and show us how we can help protect their homes.

# ENDANGERED SPECIES DAY

Every year on the third Friday in May, thousands of people around the world participate in Endangered Species Day by celebrating, learning about, and taking action to protect threatened and endangered species.

# THE WONDERS OF
# MADAGASCAR

Before we dive into meeting our animal friends, let's learn a bit about the extraordinary place they call home: Madagascar. This island is often referred to as the Great Red Island because of its rich, red soil. It's the fourth largest island in the world, sitting in the Indian Ocean, just off the coast of Africa.

Madagascar is home to an amazing array of life. Imagine an island where nearly 90% of the plants and animals can't be found anywhere else on Earth! From lush rainforests and towering baobab trees to sparkling beaches and hidden caves, this island is a paradise of diversity. But there's a dark cloud over this paradise: deforestation. Trees are being cut down for wood, farmland, and building materials, and this is a huge problem for the animals that live here. With each tree that falls, these unique creatures lose a part of their home. Over 8,000 species are in danger of vanishing forever. And that's where our adventure comes in! By learning about these amazing animals and the challenges they face, we can help spread the word and inspire others to protect them. With Aye-Eye Man guiding us, we'll discover why Madagascar's wildlife is so special and how we can be heroes for the planet.

So, as we continue our journey, keep in mind the beauty and fragility of Madagascar. Every step we take with Aye-Eye Man brings us closer to understanding how we can help preserve this incredible island for generations to come. Ready to meet some amazing animals? Let's go!

1
RED FODY
least concern

# MEET THE
# RED FODY

The vibrant Red Fody, also known as the Madagascar fody, is a striking bird with bright red feathers and black markings around its eyes. Male fodys are especially colorful while females have muted colors. These birds are about 5 inches tall and weigh up to 20 grams.

Red Fodys primarily feed on seeds and insects, but they also enjoy fruit and nectar. They prefer living in forest clearings rather than thick forests. Did you know most fodys can live 3-5 years?

## FUN FACTS

- Male Red Fodys are bright red, while females have more muted colors.
- These birds love eating seeds, insects, fruit, and nectar.
- Red Fodys typically live in open forest areas and can live up to 5 years.

2
TOMATO FROG
Near Threatened

# MEET THE
# TOMATO FROG

Our second amazing creature on this adventure is the gleaming Tomato Frog! These brilliant frogs, found only in Madagascar, are named for their vibrant reddish-orange color and their round, tomato-like shape. They can grow up to 3.5 inches, with females being a bit larger than the males.

Tomato frogs love munching on insects, larvae, and worms. When they feel threatened, they can puff up like a balloon and flash their bright colors to scare off predators. But beware— they're toxic! Did you know tomato frogs can live up to 8 years?

## FUN FACTS

- Tomato frogs thrive in the lush rainforests and swampy regions of Madagascar.
- They love stagnant ponds and slow-moving waterways.

3
FIERCE FOSSA
Vulnerable

# MEET THE
# FIERCE FOSSA

Prepare to be amazed by the mighty Fossa, the top predator of Madagascar! This cool animal is endangered, and it's always on the move, hunting both day and night. With its reddish-brown fur and sleek body, it looks like a mini cougar roaming the jungle.

The Fossa is a creature who leaps from tree to tree using its long tail for balance. It's got sharp claws and teeth, plus super senses like excellent night vision and a sharp sense of smell. And get this - Fossas can live for up to 20 years. Did you know that fossas have one or two babies a year?

## FUN FACTS

- Fossas are like the superheroes of Madagascar, keeping the jungle in balance by hunting rodents and birds.
- Even though they look like cats, Fossas are more closely related to mongooses.
- Fossas are expert climbers and can chase you up into the treetops!

4
COMET MOTH
Endangered in the wild

# MEET THE
# COMET MOTH

Get prepared to uncover the mysteries of the Comet Moth, a fascinating resident of Madagascar's rainforests. Unfortunately, this remarkable moth is endangered due to habitat loss. However, conservation efforts are underway to safeguard its future.

The males feature long, thick, feathery antennas, while the females have smaller, thinner ones. With an amazing 8-inch wingspan, the Comet Moth is one of the largest silk moths in the world. Its wings highlight amazing eyespots that resemble the glance of a fierce predator, warding off potential threats.

Did you know that adult Comet Moths only live for 4-5 days and cannot feed during this time?

## FUN FACTS

- Comet Moths spend most of their short lives surrounded by rainforest canopy.
- Bats are the biggest threat to adult Comet Moths, as they are their primary predators.
- Despite their short lifespan, Comet Moths play a crucial role in the ecosystem as pollinators.

5
PANTHER CHAMELEON
Least Concern

# MEET THE
# PANTHER CHAMELEON

Step into the world of the vibrant Panther Chameleon, a radiant reptile native to Madagascar. These remarkable creatures can grow up to 20 inches long and are famous for their ability to change colors, with different color patterns referred to as 'locales'.

Panther Chameleons are true masters of disguise, displaying shades of blue, red, green, orange, and many other vibrant colors. While males show more intense colors, females often display muted tones. In their rainforest habitat, Panther Chameleons use their lightning-fast, sticky tongues to catch insects, small birds, and other reptiles.

Did you know that despite their colorful appearance, most Panther Chameleons don't live past their first birthday in the wild, but they can live more than three years in captivity?

## FUN FACTS

- Panther Chameleons are famous for their color-changing abilities, which they use for communication and camouflage.
- Their tongues can extend more than twice the length of their bodies to catch prey.

6
RADIATED
TORTOISE
Critically Endangered

# MEET THE
# RADIATED TORTOISE

Discover the curious Radiated Tortoise, a native of Madagascar facing severe endangerment. These remarkable creatures have unique star-like markings on their shells, outlining a delightful pattern of yellow and black.

Measuring about 15 inches in length and weighing close to 20 pounds, Radiated Tortoises are herbivores, feasting on vegetation and fruit found in the forests and woodlands of Madagascar. Females can lay up to 12 eggs in a hole before departing to continue their independent lives.

Did you know that the Radiated Tortoise has an unbelievable lifespan, with some individuals living past 180 years?

## FUN FACTS

- Radiated Tortoises play a vital role in its ecosystem as seed dispersers.
- Despite their impressive lifespan, Radiated Tortoises face many threats including habitat loss and poaching.

7
GOLDEN
MANTELLA
Critically Endangered

# MEET THE
# GOLDEN MANTELLA

Let's learn about the marvelous Golden Mantella, an endangered frog species native to Madagascar. This tiny amphibian, measuring just around 1 inch in size and calls subtropical forests, moist lowlands, and tropical swamps its home. Despite its small stature, the Golden Mantella is a powerhouse of vibrant colors, flashing shades of yellow, orange, or red as a warning to potential predators of its toxic nature.

With a lifespan of about 8 years in the wild, the Golden Mantella plays a crucial role in its ecosystem. Did you know that these frogs eat small invertebrates, mites, ants, flies, and insects called collembolans?

## FUN FACTS

- Golden Mantellas lay eggs each season contributing to the next generation's survival.
- Their bright colors serve as a warning to predators to stay away.
- Despite their toxic nature, Golden Mantellas are an essential part of Madagascar's biodiversity.

8
SATANIC
LEAF-TAILED GECKO
Least concern

MEET THE

# SATANIC LEAF-TAILED GECKO

Let's uncover the secrets of the Satanic Leaf-Tailed Gecko, a fascinating creature found in Madagascar's rainforests. These unique geckos have no eyelids, relying on a thin transparent covering to protect their eyes. They use their soft, mobile tongues to keep their eyes clean from dust and debris.

Satanic Leaf-Tailed Geckos are masters of disguise, blending perfectly into their surroundings with their natural camouflage. Sticky scales under their clawed fingers and toes help them grip surfaces with ease. When threatened, they can flatten their bodies to appear leaf-like and even shed their tails to confuse predators.

Did you know that Satanic Leaf-Tailed Geckos and their rainforest habitat are endangered, making conservation efforts crucial for their survival?

## FUN FACTS

- Satanic Leaf-Tailed Geckos can live up to 10 years in the wild.
- They come in a range of colors, including brown, red, tan, blue, and white.

9
LEAF-NOSED SNAKE
least-concern

# MEET THE
# LEAF-NOSED SNAKE

Deep within Madagascar's lush rainforest, the leaf-nosed snake slithers through the undergrowth. This fascinating snake is known for its long, needle-like nose and weighs less than 2 grams. It primarily hunts lizards, frogs, and small animals.

Leaf-nosed snakes have slender bodies, reaching about 3 feet in length, with scales that blend into their surroundings in shades of yellow, brown, or gray. During the rainy season, female leaf-nosed snakes lay between 5 and 10 eggs at a time. These incredible snakes can live over 10 years in captivity. Did you know that leaf-nosed snakes are also called Spear Nosed Snakes?

## FUN FACTS

- Leaf nosed snakes are often mistaken as hanging tree branches.
- Leaf nosed snakes feed just before night begins.

# 10
## GIRAFFE WEEVIL
*Near Threatened*

# MEET THE
# GIRAFFE WEEVIL

In the forests of Madagascar lives a truly unique insect: the Giraffe Weevil. This herbivore gets its name from its remarkably long neck, which helps males in battles for territory. These insects vary in size from 15 to 90 mm and feature reddish-brown markings on their hardened wings, called elytra.

Giraffe weevils spend their days munching on leaves from the 'giraffe weevil tree' and enjoy fruits, sap, flowers, and grains. They have a short life span of just one year and face threats from birds, reptiles, and other insects. Did you know the male giraffe weevil's head is 2 to 3 times longer than the female's?

## FUN FACTS

- Giraffe Weevils eat a wide variety of plant parts.
- They have hard wings (elytra) that protect their flying wings.
- Their long necks are used for fighting other males.

11
AYE-AYE
Endangered

# MEET THE
# AYE-AYE

The Aye-aye lemur, the largest nocturnal primate on Earth, is a fascinating creature of the night. This unique lemur, standing about 2 feet tall and weighing around 4 pounds, has a furry tail longer than its body with a silver stripe down its back. With excellent hearing, sharp vision, and remarkable climbing abilities, the Aye-aye explores its rainforest habitat with ease. It uses its strange third finger to extract bugs from inside trees and its sixth finger for climbing and gripping tiny objects.

Did you know the Aye-aye is endangered and relies heavily on its unusual adaptations for survival?

## FUN FACTS

- The Aye-aye's habitat includes rainforests and cultivated areas due to deforestation.
- Its diet consists of seeds, plants, nuts, larvae, fungi, fruits, wood-boring insects, nectar, and honey.

12
BLUE COUA
least concern

# MEET THE
# BLUE COUA

The Blue Coua shines with its stunning blue feathers and distinctive oval-shaped mark around its eyes. This remarkable bird stands at about 20 inches tall and weighs up to 60 grams. Known for their unique and fascinating sounds, Blue Couas are a true delight of the rainforest.

With broad wings, large feet, and a long tail, the Blue Coua is perfectly adapted to its tropical home. During the rainy season, the females lay a single white egg. Its diet includes a variety of fruits, insects, and small reptiles found in the lush rainforest. Did you know Blue Couas prefer to jump or flop through the trees and live about seven years?

## FUN FACTS

- The Blue Coua makes unique and fascinating sounds.
- Their bright blue feathers help them blend into the lush rainforest.

# 5 steps

*to save endangered animals*

**01** Choose eco-friendly products to reduce habitat destruction.

**02** Spread awareness about endangered species.

**03** Plant trees to restore habitats.

**04** Minimize waste to decrease environmental impact on wildlife.

**05** Enforce laws to prevent deforestation.

# WORDS OF WISDOM

I'm committed to using my super powers to help protect the island of Madagascar from deforestation and habitat loss all over the world.

I believe that all species of animals have a unique role to play in keeping the earth healthy and balanced. Remember, it doesn't matter how big or small, how beautiful or weird, how mysterious or colorful each of nature's creations are, preservation of all species of animals is important. Lastly, we had an awesome informative adventure and I know for sure that Faith and Gabriella, will travel back to Big Red Island to explore more of Madagascar's unique animals.

# Our Journey of Inspiration

Ten years ago, my wife and I were blessed with the arrival of our first daughter, Faith Anne Godbold. Three years later, our second daughter, Gabriella Anne Godbold, joined our family. Both girls are not only smart, beautiful, creative, and athletic, but their kindness is truly infectious. Together, Faith and Gabriella have read over twelve hundred books and published a song titled "My Favorite Team"©.

Our daughters have always been fascinated by all species of animals, especially the weird and exotic ones. After watching several movies about the animals of Madagascar, they were inspired to do more. They decided to write and illustrate their own book to raise awareness about how deforestation affects the many species on the Great Red Island, Madagascar.

My wife and I eagerly joined in to help our girls achieve their goal of creating a children's book that focuses on threatened and endangered animals native to Madagascar.

The journey of writing this book together as a family was both fascinating and informative. Witnessing Faith and Gabriella experience their first book-writing adventure was a true pleasure. They are proud of their accomplishment and continue to take pride in being published authors, following in the footsteps of their grandfather, Elder John Lamb, and cousins, Tani Lamb and Rev. Dr. Audrey L. Turner.

# SPECIAL THANKS FROM
# FAITH & GABRIELLA

We extend our heartfelt gratitude to our incredible parents, Temico and Stephanie Godbold, for their love and support. We are also fortunate to have guidance & encouragement of our wonderful grandparents, Gail Ivory, Elder John Lamb and Valorie Lamb, and Jeffrey and Kimberly White.

A special thanks to our amazing grandmother, Susan Henke, a retired elementary school teacher and avid reader, for her invaluable pre-editing work and dedication to health and wellness. We are also grateful for the expertise and insights of our super helpful cousin, Tani Lamb, a published children's book author.

Lastly, we deeply appreciate the encouragement and support from our friends and teachers at John F. Kennedy Elementary & Dwight D. Eisenhower Middle School in Berlin, NJ. And a big thank you to our inspiration, Super Hero Aye-Eye Man.

Thank you!

# Faith &
# Gabriella

Madagascar earned its nickname "Great Red Island" because of its red colored soil.

Super sisters, Faith & Gabriella made sure to bring home a jar of Madagascar's Great Red Island's rich red soil as a token of truth proving that their adventure was a real life adventure.

# THE RED LIST CATEGORIES

**Extinct (EX):** no reasonable doubt that the last individual has died

**Extinct in the Wild (EW):** known only to survive in captivity, cultivation or well outside its natural range

**Critically Endangered (CR):** facing extremely high risk of extinction in the wild

**Endangered (EN):** facing a very high risk of extinction in the wild,

**Vulnerable (VU):** facing a high risk of extinction in the wild.

**Near Threatened (NT):** close to qualifying, or likely to qualify for a threatened category in the near future

**Least Concern (LC):** population is stable enough that it is unlikely to face extinction in the near future

**Data Deficient (DD):** not enough information on abundance or distribution to estimate its risk of extinction

# Definitions

**Adaptations**-a change or the process of change by which an organism or species becomes better

**Amphibians**-a cold-blooded vertebrate animal of a class that comprises the frogs, toads, newts and salamanders

**Array**-display or arrange things in a particular way suited to its environment

**Baobab**-a short tree with an enormous trunk and large edible fruit

**Biodiversity**-the variety of life in the world or in a particular habitat or ecosystem

**Camouflage**-hide or disguise the presence of (a person, animal, or object) by means of camouflage

**Carnivore**-an organism that eats meat

**Crucial**-of great importance

**Cultivated area-**land that is used to grow crops

**Debris**-scattered pieces of waste or remains

**Deforestation**-the action of clearing a wide area of trees

**Departing**-leave, especially in order to start a journey

**Disguises**-give a different appearance in order to conceal one's identity

**Distinctive**-marking as separate or different

**Eco-friendly products**-products not harmful to the environment

**Ecosystem**-a biological community of Interacting organisms and their physical environment

**Elytra**-each of the two wing cases of a beetle

**Embark**-begin a course of action, especially one that is important or demanding

**Environmental impact**- defined as any change to the environment

**Exotic**-mysteriously different or unusual

**Fascinating**-drawing irresistible attention and interest of someone

**Fierce-**having or displaying an intense or ferocious aggressiveness

**Forrest clearing**-the process by which vegetation, trees, bushes, and roots are permanently removed

**Fragility**-a state of being delicate or breakable

**Gleaming**-reflecting light, typically very clean or polished

**Herbivore**-an animal that feeds on plants

**Impressive**-evoking admiration through size, quality, or skill; grand, imposing, or awesome

**Intense colors**-a highly intense color is bright and a low-intensity color is more neutral or muted

**Lifecycle**-the series of changes in the life of an organism including reproduction

**Locales-**change colors, with different color patterns

**Lush**-vegetation growing in "lush greenery and cultivated fields"

**Marvelous**-extremely good or pleasing

**Muted hue**-subtle colors that are not bright

**Nocturnal primate**-active during the night

**Pollinator**-an insect or other agent that carries pollen to a plant and allows fertilization

**Primarily**-for the most part, mostly or usually

**Remarkable-**worthy of attention

**Resident**-lives somewhere permanently or on a long-term basis

**Safe guard**-a precautionary measure warding off impending danger or damage or injury

**Sleek**-smooth and glossy hair, fur, or skin

**Stagnant**-motionless water, not flowing in a stream or current

**Stature**-physical makeup

**Stewardship**-the job of supervising or taking care of something, such as an organization or property

**Striking**-attracting attention by reason of being unusual, extreme, or prominent

**Stunning**-extremely impressive or attractive

**Subtropical**-bordering on the tropics; nearly tropical

**Threatened**-to cause someone or something to be vulnerable or at risk; endanger

**Thrive**-to grow vigorously

**Transparent**-allowing light to pass through so that objects behind can be seen

**Toxic**-poisonous

**Unique**-being the only one of its kind; unlike anything else

**Vanishing**-disappear suddenly and completely

**Vibrant**-full of color, energy and enthusiasm

**Vital**-absolutely necessary or important; essential

# References


- **Aye-Aye**

  https://en.wikipedia.org/wiki/Aye-aye
- **Blue Coua**

  https://www.oiseaux-birds.com/card-blue-coua.html#:~:text=The%20Blue%20Coua%20is%20not,it%20is%20not%20globally%20threatened.
  https://en.wikipedia.org/wiki/Blue_coua
  https://animalia.bio/blue-coua?category=3
- **Comet Moth**

  https://en.wikipedia.org/wiki/Comet_moth
  https://www.nhm.ac.uk/discover/spotlight-madagascan-moon-moth.html
- **Fossa**

  https://en.wikipedia.org/wiki/Fossa_(animal)
  https://www.nationalgeographic.com/animals/mammals/facts/fossa
- **Giraffe Weevil**

  https://en.wikipedia.org/wiki/Giraffe_weevil
  https://www.sfzoo.org/giraffe-weevil/
- **Golden Mantel**

  https://animalia.bio/golden-mantella
  https://en.wikipedia.org/wiki/Golden
- **Leaf-Nosed Snake**

  https://en.wikipedia.org/wiki/Langaha_madagascariensis
  https://www.madamagazine.com/en/die-blattnasennatter-2/
- **Madagascar's Deforestation**

  https://www.worldwildlife.org/places/madagascar
  https://en.wikipedia.org/wiki/Deforestation_in_Madagascar
  https://www.theguardian.com/environment/2023/jan/10/madagascar-unique-wildlife-extinction-aoe
  https://wwfeu.awsassets.panda.org/downloads/madagascar_forest_cc_final_12nov07.pdf
- **Panther Chamelon**

  https://en.wikipedia.org/wiki/Panther_chameleon
  https://animalia.bio/panther-chameleon
  https://reptilesmagazine.com/panther-chameleon-care
- **Radiated Tortoise**

  https://en.wikipedia.org/wiki/Radiated_tortoise
- **Red Fody**

  https://en.wikipedia.org/wiki/Red_fody
  https://invasives.org.za/fact-sheet-animals/red-fody/
  https://animalia.bio/red-fody
- **Satanic Leaf Tail Gecko**

  https://en.wikipedia.org/wiki/Uroplatus_phantasticus
  https://animalia.bio/satanic-leaf-tailed-gecko
  https://factanimal.com/satanic-leaf-tailed-gecko/
- **The Red list Categories**

  https://www.birdlife.org/news/2022/02/08/7-things-you-might-have-missed-from-the-2021-red-list-update/
- **Tomato Frog**

  https://nationalzoo.si.edu/animals/tomato-frog
  https://en.wikipedia.org/wiki/Tomato_frog
  https://en.m.wikipedia.org/wiki/Tomato_frog#:~:text=The%20lifespan%20of%20the%20tomato,reach%204%20inches%20in%20length.
- **Aye-aye Super-Hero**

  Super Hero Aye-Eye Man©
  Super Hero Aye-Eye©

BLUE ♥ COUA

By:

AYe-aye
By: Aye-Eye-Man superhero
Gue


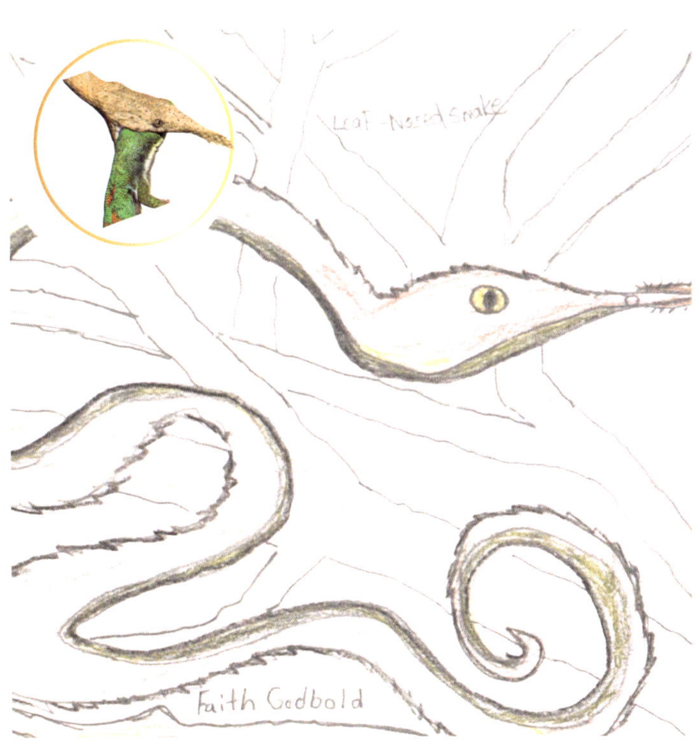

Leaf-Nosed snake
Faith Godbold

Golden mantela

Tomato frog

Radiated Tortie
By: Faith
Comet Moth
By: Aye-Eye-Man
Super Hero
Panther Chameleon